MW01106211

A Principal's Expectations from A-Z...

A Student Success Guide for School & Life

**Written and Edited by
Ms. Deniece M. Fields, M.Ed.**

**Foreword by
Bishop Charles H. McClelland**

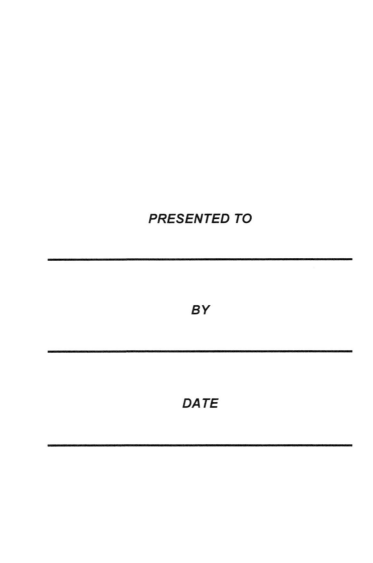

PRESENTED TO

_____

BY

_____

DATE

_____

Foreword written by Bishop C.H. McClelland

"A Principal's Expectations from A to Z..."
(for students)

A Student Success Guide
for School & Life

---

*Invaluable Insights from an
Urban Educator, Leader, Motivator,
and Speaker...*

Written and Edited by
Deniece M. Fields, M. Ed.

Coming Soon:

~Coming 2016~

"A Principal's Expectations
from A to Z..."
(for teachers)

~Coming 2017~

"A Principal's Expectations
from A to Z..."
(for parents)

~Coming 2018~

"I Know Who I Am..." – My Bio

Foreword written by Bishop C.H. McClelland

"A Principal's Expectations from A to Z..." (for students)

A Student Success Guide
for School & Life

Written and Edited by
Deniece M. Fields, M. Ed.

Portions of *A Principal's Expectations from A-Z...for Students* were originally published as *A Principal's Expectations from A-Z* (St. Louis, Missouri 2013)

ISBN 978-0-692-45410-7

Published in association with Ingramspark, www.ingramspark.com

Printed and bound in the United States of America

THIS BOOK IS DEDICATED TO...

- My students from *Grand Avenue Middle School*
  (Milwaukee, WI)

- My students from the *Milwaukee Urban League Academy of Business & Economics - MULABE*
  (Milwaukee, WI)

- My students from *Confluence Academy - Old North Campus*
  (St. Louis, MO)

- My students from the *Young Women's Leadership Charter School of Chicago*
  (Chicago, IL)

- EVERY student who needs to be reminded of their GREATNESS...
  (All Over the World...)

- My Nephews – **Lance N. Fields & Kylan H. Fields** whom I LOVE dearly!!!!!!!!!!!!

- ALL of My Cousins...

Table of Contents...

-Never settle for mediocrity-40

-Overload yourselves with knowledge and skills-43

-Passionately speak to what you believe-46

-Question those things for which you need answers

-Remember the right: Release the wrong-52

-Speak so people will listen-55

-Train your minds to receive positive thoughts-58

-Utilize those in your life who can help you move forward-61

-Visualize yourself being the top in everything you do-64

-Wait for the right opportunities-67

-X out haters-70

-Instead of asking "Y" me, say "Y" not me?-74

-Zestfully walk into your next phase of life being proud of who you are-77

Foreword

Ms. Deniece M. Fields has captured the essence of excellence for anyone serious about *"being their Best"* in the pursuit of achieving any goal in life that they choose. Deniece has managed to both simplify and clarify, in a very pointed and profound way in her book, what steps are necessary for anyone who chooses to rise above the mundane mediocrity of the "status quo".

What I find most impressive about this book are the author's personal experiences, skills and attitude she shares with her readers.

As her Pastor, I saw her leadership skills early on as a young woman starting college with a passion for young people, especially our young women. Ms. Fields is a mentor and role model who believes strongly in education and understands firsthand many of the challenges the youth face. Her experience as a Youth Leader, Teacher, Educator, Principal and Executive Director has brought her to where she is today, and into achieving the goals she set early in her life. Furthermore, to *practice* the principles that she shares in her book, will undoubtedly improve interpersonal relationships with others, whether in the public or private arena. Everything we do in life is connected to our relationships with other people, and the experiences we find ourselves involved in with them. We must always remember that we are not defined by what others say, or even do, to us, but rather by what we believe and say about ourselves, remembering that *"no one can make you feel inferior without your consent."*

Ms. Fields is an excellent speaker, presenter, and motivator. When she shares, you can tell that she is passionate, anointed, and filled with the wisdom of her Maker. Because of her transparency through the experiences of her own personal life, interaction working with leaders, business owners, and youth over the years, she has learned and knows what works.

This book is a must read for every Student, Educator, Leader, and anyone serious about experiencing your *best life and fulfilling your God-Given purpose!*

I count myself to be very blessed and privileged to serve as Pastor to Ms. Deniece Fields, a team player, and team leader with a proven track record of achievement in Education, as well as inspiring thousands of youth to be their *Best.*

~Pastor C.H. McClelland
Wisconsin Northwest Jurisdictional Bishop

ACKNOWLEDGEMENTS...

To all of my Principals:
~Mr. John Schmul. MacDowell Montessori~
~Dr. Rogers Onick. Samuel Morse Middle School~
~Mr. Willie Jude. James Madison High School~

Thank you for being memorable and walking in a way
that **LEADERS** should walk! I remember each of you
vividly...along with the lessons each of you taught me...

To my childhood Pastors:
~Pastor Russell B. Williamson. Zion Hill M.B.C.~
~Pastor and First Lady Abraham (RIP) & Gladys
Mack. New Paradise M.B.C.~

Thank you for recognizing the **LEADER** in me at an
early age and allowing me to serve in Leadership roles
as a child...

To my Bishop & My Pastor:
~Bishop Charles H. McClelland.
Holy Cathedral COGIC~

Thank you for being YOU in the lives of so many
people. a true **LEADER** and Man of God, who
understands Leadership and exemplifies Leadership
in your daily walk. Thank you for valuing Education
and for continuing to stand up for Education from the
pulpit. Thank you for your willingness to write the
Foreword for "A Principal's Expectations from A-Z...for
students" Your continued prayers, teaching, support
and encouragement have meant so much to me and I
am forever grateful to God for leading me to your
ministry. It has been a TRUE BLESSING!

SPECIAL THANKS...

- To my Wonderful Parents. Mr. and Mrs. LeRoy & Deborah Fields. Sr. **THANK YOU** for doing your ABSOLUTE BEST to make me who I am today...I LOVE YOU TO LIFE!!!

- To the Love of My Life. Mr. William Polite. **THANK YOU** for encouraging me to turn my written piece into a book. Your continued support has meant the world to me!

- To My Cousin. Olivia Fields. **THANK YOU** for pushing me every time we talked. by asking me. "What's up with the book???"

- To My Best Friend. Charletta Lloyd. **THANK YOU** for always believing in me and knowing that I would always do whatever I said I would do and always reminding me of God's work in my life!

Introduction

This book was written to encourage every student (anyone who is still ready and willing to LEARN=everyone) whose hands it will touch. Everything you read is something you may have heard from a teacher or from a principal. These are words that I've shared with all of my students over the years. Each time I close a speech. I close with "A Principal's Expectations from A-Z..." and people of all ages are intrigued. People throughout the United States of America have shared with me that they keep a copy on their refrigerator, on their mirror, in their office, or just in their belongings to serve as a reminder that we all need to be encouraged to be the absolute best we can be each and every day! Enjoy and pass it on! Be a blessing to someone else today!

Adjust your attitude to reflect the positive young man/woman you are meant to be...

"People may hear your words, but they feel your attitude." ~John C. Maxwell

[1]

Have you ever heard the phrase. "Your attitude determines your altitude"? Believe me. it is one of the most accurate statements you will ever hear. A bad attitude will shut doors. cut you off. and hinder opportunities. Nobody likes a funky attitude...nobody. It is the quickest way to lose support in school and in life. You may have difficulty reading. writing. and computing. but with the right attitude. you can still succeed!

Remember this: "If you continue to do what you've always done. you'll always get what you've always gotten." If you are stagnant and not moving forward the way you would like. check your attitude. It may be the difference between your next opportunity and your next opposition.

Ask yourself:

- ♦ Does my attitude change when I'm at school? For better or for worse?
- ♦ Does my attitude change when I am around certain people? For better or for worse?
- ♦ Does my attitude attract others? What types of people do I attract?

My Commitment: _____

_____

_____

_____

_____

_____

_____

_____

_____

_____

_____

_____

_____

_____

_____

_____

_____

_____

_____

_____

_____

_____

_____

[3]

$\mathcal{B}$

Believe that you are capable of doing anything...

"Belief in oneself is one of the most important bricks in building any successful venture." ~Lydia M. Child

[4]

"Sometimes you have to believe in someone else's belief in you until your own kicks in". This is for those of you who struggle with believing you can do ANYTHING! Surround yourself with people who will remind you that you are capable of succeeding at whatever you desire. not those who always have reasons. better yet. "excuses" as to why you can't succeed. Once you truly believe that you are capable and have the same rights and capabilities as anyone else. everything is within your reach...

Think about all of the people who have told you what you cannot do or what you are not going to do when it comes to living out your dreams...write their names down (right now)...post them to serve as a reminder to GET AWAY FROM THEM AS QUICKLY AS YOU POSSIBLY CAN!

You CAN get to school on time. You CAN study more than just 15 minutes a night. You CAN finish high school. You CAN get into and through college! You CAN speak in front of others! You CAN do all that you desire. if you only believe...

Ask yourself:

+ What do I enjoy doing?
+ What do I do well?
+ How did I become successful at these things?
+ How can I continue to build on these successes?

My commitment: _____

_____

_____

_____

_____

_____

_____

_____

_____

_____

_____

_____

_____

_____

_____

C

Carry yourself as a young man/young woman at all times...

"If you do not value yourself, it will show. Always wear your invisible crown." ~Author unknown

Refrain from being predictable. Too often, you are looked at in a negative light based on the way you carry yourself in public places. Avoid being loud, rude, and disrespectful, but instead, always speak with respect, and never use profanity.

Whether you're on public transit, in restaurants, at the movie theatre, or in the mall, don't wait to show out in public places for the sake of trying to impress your peers. In the long run, you make yourself, your family, and anything/anyone you represent look ridiculous.

Be the person others want to follow – a strong, courageous, mature, respectable, and positively influential young LEADER.

Ask yourself:

- Am I a fair and true representation of my school, my Leaders, my family, and myself?
- Would my public actions earn me a job with a possible future employer who may be watching me?

✦ Who am I trying to impress? Who <u>should</u> I
   try to impress? Why?

My Commitment: _____

_____

_____

_____

_____

_____

_____

_____

_____

_____

_____

_____

_____

_____

_____

_____

_____

_____

_____

Demand respect as you deliver respect...

"There is no respect for others without humility in one's self." ~Henri Frederic Amiel

[10]

Teachers love respectful children...ask any teacher you've ever had and they will tell you the same...they love respectful children. In the most difficult circumstances. challenging classes. low. test scores. or overwhelming responsibilities. you will always receive the support that you need when you are respectful.

You must also demand respect. Although teachers don't owe you anything. you have the right to be recognized and respected. In the words of the legendary. Merri Dee: "Know your name. and only answer to that name. Do not allow anyone to call you anything other than your name." It was given to you for a reason. along with the high level of dignity and respect that you deserve.

Have a commanding presence – strong voice. great eye contact. and a confident. but humble spirit that speaks respect for self. while respecting those in authority.

Ask yourself:

+ What does respect look like. sound like. and feel like?

- How do I consistently demonstrate respect?
- Based on who I am today, what legacy will I leave?

My Commitment: _____

_____

_____

_____

_____

_____

_____

_____

_____

_____

_____

_____

_____

_____

_____

_____

_____

_____

_____

_____

Exemplify greatness...

"Think like a queen (or king). A queen (or king) is not afraid to fail. Failure is another steppingstone to greatness." ~Oprah Winfrey

[13]

It's okay...You are destined for greatness! Why is it that growing up, it's GREAT to be the GREATEST student in the class or in the school, but by the time you reach middle and high school, it suddenly becomes embarrassing to be GREAT??? It's not embarrassing...If you think it is, change your mindset!

Compete for the attention of your teachers, not your peers! Show what you know and demonstrate your desire to learn as much as you can. So many great leaders have come and gone, so now we are waiting for the next generation of great leaders to step up!

If you want better, you have to know better. Once you know better, you have to do better. Exemplify what it truly means to be GREAT! It's in you!

Ask yourself:

- Am I one of the next GREAT LEADERS?
- What have I done to be the next GREAT LEADER?
- How am I preparing myself to be the next GREAT LEADER?

My Commitment: _____

_____

_____

_____

_____

_____

_____

_____

_____

_____

_____

_____

_____

_____

_____

_____

_____

_____

_____

_____

_____

_____

_____

_F_orget those who
falsely accuse you of
being someone less
than who you really
are...

"A clear conscience laughs at false accusations."
~Author unknown

Oh, yes!!!!! There will forever be people who falsely accuse you. They're not going anywhere! In fact, the more successful you become, the more they appear...Don't allow them to define you! It is important to recognize those people when you see them and keep them close to you so you can stay several steps ahead of them. No matter how tough things may seem, never let them change who you are.

It is difficult to see the positive in people when they look for the negative in you, but DO NOT LET THEM WIN! This is always much easier said than done, but you can handle it. It's not you, it's them. This is a situation that all people have gone through, are going through, or will go through... Just remember...What you do is more important than what they say!

Ask yourself:

- How much of what people say about me is really true?
- Who are these false accusers?
- Am I the same person wherever I go?
- What will people see? What will people say?

My Commitment: _____

_____

_____

_____

_____

_____

_____

_____

_____

_____

_____

_____

_____

_____

_____

_____

_____

_____

_____

_____

_____

_____

_____

Gladly accept the challenges you will face...

"We don't grow when things are easy; we grow when we face challenges." ~Joyce Meyer

[19]

My Pastor, Bishop Charles H. McClelland, always reminds us, "Without a test, you have no testimony". This is true. Embrace the challenges as they come. Weak people run from challenges, mediocre people blame others for their challenges, but strong people face, accept, and overcome their challenges.

No one likes to wait, no one likes to hurt, and no one likes to lose. Unfortunately, you feel one these emotions when you're in a challenging situation. You may not believe it at the time, but your hard work, your dedication, and your perseverance will always pay off. In the end, you will always come out stronger, but you must stay in the race and you must finish!

Ask yourself:

- ◆ What is the biggest challenge I've ever faced?
- ◆ What challenge do I foresee and am I prepared?
- ◆ What lesson am I supposed to learn from this challenge?

My Commitment: _____

_____
_____
_____
_____
_____
_____
_____
_____
_____
_____
_____
_____
_____
_____
_____
_____
_____
_____
_____
_____
_____
_____
_____
_____

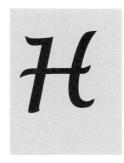

Honor those who want the best for you...

"You can burn bridges, but Honor can never be breached." ~Esteb "Scoobz" Guye

[22]

Don't fight authority....you will NEVER win! Extremely successful students are those who listen to the guidance of those in authority...teachers, leaders, mentors, and parents. Proverbs 1:7 says, "Only fools despise wisdom." Do not fall into that trap! Honor and adhere to wise council. Your teachers, your leaders, your mentors, and your parents want the best for you!

How do you really know who TRULY wants the BEST for you? Pay attention to what they EXPECT of you... If you have a teacher who gives you a grade instead of making you earn your grade, question if they really want the best for you. If you are in a school where the administrators have instructed teachers "not to give failing grades to anyone under any circumstance", question if they really want the best for you. Why? When you have teachers who work you until you know the material, work you until you master the material, and work you until you are able to teach the material to someone else, you have a teacher who TRULY cares about you and your success. It is rather difficult to explain to a college how you have a 4.0 grade point average, with a 15 ACT score...they are going to ask, "How can this be?"

Your work, your grades, your efforts...must be consistent with each other.

Remember this...the teacher who works your nerves, makes you cry, and makes you redo what you've turned in if it is below standard, is the teacher you will always remember...for the right reasons! You will appreciate them later!

Choose your team wisely! Listen to those who are in a position to help you, teach you, and guide you. Again, do not fight them...you will NEVER win!

Ask yourself:

- ✛ Who are the people I am fighting?
- ✛ Who are the people I respect?
- ✛ How can I fix my broken relationships and start over?

My Commitment: _____

_____

_____

_____

_____

_____

_____

I

Independently make decisions that will be beneficial, not a hindrance...

"Decisions are the hardest moves to make, especially when it's a choice between what you want and what is right." ~Author Unknown

Be a LEADER! Make your own decisions and do not sway! Every decision you make today will determine your tomorrow. Drinking, smoking, and other "fun activity" will have a negative effect on you in the long run. Every "kickback or house party" is not suitable for you. Life is too short, eternity is too long, and after the fact is too late to find out you made mistakes that were influenced by other people's decision.

Being a young adult can be tough...people trust you to be able to make your own decisions...wise decisions, but your peers can be very influential as they stand on the sideline watching and waiting to see you fall with them. Although the best decisions are not always the popular decisions, they are always the right decisions!

Ask yourself:

- Am I happy with the person I am today?
- Where do I want to be in 10 years?
- Are the decisions I'm making today preparing me for success in the next 10 years of my life?

My Commitment: _____

_____

_____

_____

_____

_____

_____

_____

_____

_____

_____

_____

_____

_____

_____

_____

_____

_____

_____

_____

_____

_____

_____

_____

Join with those who share the same vision...

"Vision is the art of seeing what is invisible to others."
~Jonathan Swift

[28]

All company is not good company...don't waste time around people whose vision does not match yours or who cannot help you realize and/or carry out yours. Surround yourself with those who are serious about education, serious about life, and serious about success.

During this process, you will lose people who you may have considered your friends, but it's okay...you'll get over it and so will they. When you're headed up and moving forward, those who support you are those you want around. Those who do not support you are those you'll be happy to leave behind...

Ask yourself:

- Who are my real/true supporters? How do I know?
- What is my plan to break away from those who do not share my vision for success?
- Am I okay with standing alone and leaving certain people behind?

My Commitment: _____

_____

_____

_____

_____

_____

_____

_____

_____

_____

_____

_____

_____

_____

_____

_____

_____

_____

_____

_____

_____

_____

_____

Know who you are, and what you stand for...

"Never forget who/what you are. for surely the world will not." ~George R.R. Martin

Know who you are, whose you are, and what you stand for. Your name, your character, and your reputation should carry good weight. When you respect who you are, others will do the same, and if they don't, you must teach them how to treat you. Know your value and know your worth.

During your teen and young adult years, you are pressured to say things, do things, and be someone other than the person you are supposed to be. Do not be tricked! Remember this... "If you don't stand for something, you fall for anything."

If you are to be who you really are ALL of the time, make sure you are proud of who you really are ALL of the time...

Ask yourself:

- ⚔ When people see me, who do they see?
- ⚔ When people hear about me, what do they think?
- ⚔ Who am I? What do I represent?

[32]

My Commitment: _____

_____

_____

_____

_____

_____

_____

_____

_____

_____

_____

_____

_____

_____

_____

_____

_____

_____

_____

_____

_____

_____

_____

_____

_____

L

Look forward and Leave negative mess behind...

"Life is about moving on. accepting changes and looking forward to what makes you stronger and more complete." ~Author Unknown

[34]

Messy people love company. Your name should never come up in other people's drama. You never want to be found gossiping about others, agreeing with those who are putting other people down, or laughing at someone's misfortunes.

When you realize that someone in your circle is that type of person, immediately correct that person or separate yourself. I guarantee...you'll always feel better and look better when people know you for NOT being involved in negative mess!

Ask yourself:

- When mess begins, where am I?
- Whether I'm present or not, when conversations take place, where does my name fit...if anywhere?
- Do I realize that those who gossip about others, probably gossip about me too?
- Am I known for being a person who will always defend what is right?

My Commitment: _____

_____

_____

_____

_____

_____

_____

_____

_____

_____

_____

_____

_____

_____

_____

_____

_____

_____

_____

_____

_____

_____

Mean what you say &
say what you mean...

"When you don't keep your word, you lose credibility."
~Robin Sharma

[37]

If you don't mean it, don't say it... Often times, you are coerced into doing/saying things that you really don't mean for the sake of impressing others. This strategy will always get you caught up.

Recognize that your word is your word and should be kept. When you mean what you say and say what you mean, people attribute that to your character. People who say things but don't mean them are seen as having a character flaw. A person with good character takes the time to think about what they say before they say it, acknowledges other's feeling before saying something that may be hurtful or offensive, and stands firm on what they say because they are confident that they are speaking wisdom and not foolery.

Ask yourself:

- How important is it to me that I always stand on my word?
- How much credibility does my word hold?
- Do people believe what I say when I say it?

My Commitment: _____

_____

_____

_____

_____

_____

_____

_____

_____

_____

_____

_____

_____

_____

_____

_____

_____

_____

_____

_____

_____

_____

_____

_____

_____

_____

Never settle for mediocrity...

"Be fearful of mediocrity..." ~Jonathan Ellery

Doing just enough is never enough. Successful people never settle; they are too busy trying to see what else can be done and how to improve what's already been accomplished. If you want to stand out from the rest, you have to be willing to do more than anyone else, more than what you did before, and more than expected.

Too often, students do not get ahead because they are too lazy, too busy on social media, or too busy trying to impress people. Don't take shortcuts – they only allow for temporary wins. You want long-term success. This type of success is only achieved by believing you are far beyond mediocre.

Ask yourself:

- Am I giving all that I can in school and in life?
- Do I stand out from my peers? In what way?
- How consistent am I in my pursuit of success?

My Commitment: _____

_____

_____

_____

_____

_____

_____

_____

_____

_____

_____

_____

_____

_____

_____

_____

_____

_____

_____

_____

_____

_____

_____

_____

_____

Overload yourself with knowledge & skills...

"Never stop learning. because life never stops teaching." ~Author Unknown

[43]

Learn! Learn! Learn some more! "Get all you can and can all you get!" Whether you enjoy learning by reading or learning by doing, you must learn all you can, while you can. Employers want employees who are intelligent and/or hardworking. Meeting both of these expectations is ideal, but at very minimal, you must be one or the other.

Being well-rounded in what you do and in what you know are going to be key factors in how far you will go. One of the greatest feelings in the world is being chosen based on your skills, knowledge, experience, or expertise. When others are passed up due to their limited or lack of qualifications, but you are chosen to do the job because of your previous accomplishments, at that moment, you become appreciative of the hard work and sacrifice you put in on the days you wanted to quit. Don't allow fear to keep you from asking questions and don't allow laziness to keep you from reading another sentence, another chapter, or another book!

Ask yourself:

- ✚ In what area(s) do I feel most comfortable and in what area(s) do I need to learn/grow?
- ✚ Do I know how to find the answers to what I don't know?
- ✚ Am I confident in what I do know so that I am not ashamed of what I don't know?
- ✚ How can I push myself to do more and learn more?

My Commitment: _____

_____

_____

_____

_____

_____

_____

_____

_____

_____

_____

_____

_____

_____

Passionately speak to what you believe...

"Passion makes you pursue your purpose" ~Deniece Fields

Follow your heart and speak from it. People can clearly tell when you are feeding them fluff, not being truthful, or just talking for the sake of talking. If you truly believe in something, when you speak on it, the passion you have for it will be obvious and you will earn a phenomenal amount of respect for it.

No one has to make you do something you are passionate about doing. You get up and do it willingly and with enthusiasm! You are driven, you are determined, and you recognize the possibilities ahead of you.

If you continue to live your life with passion, you will have no regrets!

Ask yourself:

- What makes me laugh? What makes me cry?
- What keeps me awake?
- What am I passionate about? How do I know, and how do others know?

My Commitment: _____

_____

_____

_____

_____

_____

_____

_____

_____

_____

_____

_____

_____

_____

_____

_____

_____

_____

_____

_____

_____

_____

_____

_____

_____

Question those things for which you need answers...

"By doubting we are led to question, by questioning we arrive at the truth." ~Peter Abelard

Some people will not expect you to ask questions. Ask them anyway! Some people don't want you to ask questions. Ask them anyway! Don't let other people hush your mouth. Find your voice and use it! "Be comfortable with what you know, so you're rarely uncomfortable with what you don't know..." ~Deniece Fields

When you ask questions and get clear understanding, you are continuing to build your confidence. One reason some children are so much smarter than others, is because they began asking questions as soon as they were old enough to talk. Being inquisitive will serve as an asset to your continued growth. "In all your getting, get an understanding..."

Ask yourself:

- How confident am I?
- Do I always ask questions when I am unclear?
- Is my ability or comfort with asking questions determined by who's sitting in the room?

↓ How can I build my confidence to a point where I am never afraid to ask questions for clarity?

My Commitment: _____

_____

_____

_____

_____

_____

_____

_____

_____

_____

_____

_____

_____

_____

_____

_____

_____

_____

_____

_____

_____

_____

Remember the right;
Release the wrong...

"Wrong is wrong even if everyone is doing it. Right is right even if no one is doing it."

[52]

Keep your mind focused on all of the things you've done right and do not let the wrong thoughts take over. Making mistakes is a part of life and we all make them. The biggest mistake that people make is to keep dwelling on the wrong and allowing it to hinder their progress. Let it go!

Your past hurt will only affect your future if you allow it. Allow every mistake to serve as a teaching tool. When you say, "If I could do it all over again, I would do it differently," you should move forward, then do it. Create the opportunity to do it right! The purpose of growing is to learn and become better, not bitter. Instead of keeping track of your mistakes and the mistakes of others, keep up with your successes and the encouragement you receive from others. You will be pleased with the results!

Ask yourself:

- What am I still holding on to that is causing me pain? How can I release it?
- What lesson was I supposed to learn from my past mistakes?
- Am I allowing past hurt to hinder my growth and my relationships with others?

[53]

✛ What are the positives I have encountered just this week? How can I remain focused on these things and move forward?

My Commitment: _____

_____

_____

_____

_____

_____

_____

_____

_____

_____

_____

_____

_____

_____

_____

_____

_____

_____

_____

_____

S

Speak so people will listen...

"You have to speak your dream out loud."   ~Kelly
Corrigan

[55]

People love listening to those who have something to say...not those who just enjoy talking to hear themselves talk. Do not dominate the conversations trying to be impressive, but instead, listen attentively and wait to respond. Figure out where your point fits in and make sure you state it clearly. You will be able to tell if people are buying in to what you are saying...they will smile, nod, and often agree. If people roll their eyes, keep their head down working on something else, or stare at others while you're speaking, chances are...they aren't listening or they're tired of listening to you. There may be times when people are staring at you while you're speaking, but giving no expression at all. Don't be alarmed. This may mean that you have really captured their attention and they are in deep thought. Now, it's your responsibility to keep their attention!

Some of the best feedback/comments you can receive after you speak are: "I always look forward to hearing you speak! I really enjoy listening to you! When YOU speak, I listen!"

Ask yourself:

- Do people look forward to hearing me speak?
- Do people enjoy hearing me speak?
- Do people listen and take note of what I am saying? How do I know?

My Commitment: _____

_____

_____

_____

_____

_____

_____

_____

_____

_____

_____

_____

_____

_____

_____

_____

_____

_____

_____

_____

Train your mind to receive positive thoughts...

"Nothing changes until you change. Everything changes, once you change." ~Author Unknown

[58]

You really *are* more powerful than you think! When you spend time thinking on all of the negative things you encounter on a daily basis, you can't help but to become bitter, depressed, and hard to be around. The only people who will enjoy being around you are those who are just as depressing or as depressed as you. But, when you begin to tell yourself how GREAT you are, how BEAUTIFUL you are, and how ACCOMPLISHED you are, you walk with more confidence!

Often times, people will blame someone else or something else for the negative thoughts they have from day to day. The truth is, no one can control your thoughts but you! You have to start believing that what you think and what you believe is a total reflection of who you will become.

Ask yourself:

- Who do I <u>see</u> in the mirror each day?
- What do I <u>say</u> about the person in the mirror each day?
- What do I <u>think</u> about the person in the mirror each day?

My Commitment: _____

_____

_____

_____

_____

_____

_____

_____

_____

_____

_____

_____

_____

_____

_____

_____

_____

_____

_____

_____

_____

_____

_____

_____

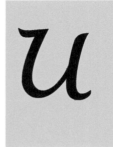

Utilize those in your life who can help you move forward...

"If your presence can't add value to my life. your absence will make no difference." ~Author Unknown

Be smart and take the advice of those who know best. In the words of my Pastor, Bishop C.H. McClelland, "Going There can't tell Been There how to Get There..." But, those who have already walked the route you're walking know a little more than you think. Don't allow your pride to get in the way of sound advice. Listening to the wrong advice will send you backwards and cause you to take a number of steps over and over again, but utilizing those who can help you move forward will teach you how to navigate through life learning the best routes without having to repeat them. Don't burn bridges...build solid relationships...and value longevity with great people. You will always need someone else as you travel through your journey of life.

Ask yourself:

- ✦ Who do I have in my pocket right now that serves as a resource for me?
- ✦ What advice have they given me that can help me move forward?
- ✦ When was the last time I spoke to them or dropped them an email?

⬥ How comfortable am I reaching out and making new connections? How can I continue to build my network of resources?

My Commitment: _____

_____

_____

_____

_____

_____

_____

_____

_____

_____

_____

_____

_____

_____

_____

_____

_____

_____

_____

_____

_____

_____

Visualize yourself being the top in everything you do...

"You can seize only what you can see." ~John C. Maxwell

There is absolutely nothing wrong with encouraging yourself! As a matter fact...YOU SHOULD!

As you strive towards reaching the top in everything you do. you will have people who will say. "You think you're so much...", "You think you're so great...", or "You want to be such a big shot..." When people say these things to you. say. "I am much...I am great...I am a big shot."

Speak life into your existence...EVERYDAY! Call out what it is you wish to become...EVERYDAY! Don't think as small-minded people think. but instead. think big. dream big. and DO it big...EVERYDAY!

Never set low expectations...especially for yourself! When you see others who have reached the top. ask yourself. "What did they do and how did they do it?" Ask them how they did it and learn from them. Then. figure out how you will accomplish and surpass that goal for yourself! If they did it. why can't you? You can and you will!

Ask yourself:

- Am I afraid of success?
- Can I handle being at the top?

[65]

+ Am I worried about what others will say or
  think once I reach the top?

My Commitment: _____

_____
_____
_____
_____
_____
_____
_____
_____
_____
_____
_____
_____
_____
_____
_____
_____
_____
_____
_____
_____
_____
_____
_____
_____

<u>W</u>ait for the right opportunities...

"N.O. = Next Opportunity" ~Author Unknown

Although "opportunities" are great, you have to make sure that you choose the "right opportunity", the one that best fits you. As a student, you will be offered many different opportunities, but as you grow, you will have to determine which are advantageous and which are roadblocks.

Weigh all of your options. Think long-term success, not temporary fixes. Look at the entire picture, not just the pieces you want to see. Do not rush or jump into just anything. Review it, question it, observe it, and pray on it. If it's for you, it's for you, and you will know it.

Ask yourself:

- Who supports me/my decisions 100%?
- Who tells me the truth, whether I want to hear it or not?
- Can I handle the truth? Am I ready to accept that which I don't really want to accept?
- Who do I seek out for advice?

My Commitment: _____

_____

_____

_____

_____

_____

_____

_____

_____

_____

_____

_____

_____

_____

_____

_____

_____

_____

_____

_____

_____

_____

_____

_____

_____

X out haters...
X out haters...
X out haters...

"Don't worry about those who talk behind your back.
they're behind you for a reason." ~Author Unknown

Oooohhh yes! The haters are out there and they're waiting to come after you! Once it begins, it never ends... One of the most difficult parts of being successful is dealing with those who can't handle your success. The good news is that you will certainly learn how to handle them!

Know this...no matter how hard you work, no matter what you do to become more successful, and no matter how much you help others, jealous people will always look for ways to tear you down. It's rather unfortunate, but it's often the reality.

You will have people who smile with you and seem to be happy for you, but turn around and speak negatively about you to others. You have those who are inconsistent with their applause for you and act as if they didn't realize it. Then, you have those who will blatantly ignore you and your successes, never commend you, and follow up with lies about you to your supporters. When it first happens, you will be shocked, confused, and even hurt. As time goes on, you will become better equipped to handle the hurt, but it will always be a test. It's not too difficult when your haters are those you don't know, the problem is when it becomes those you do know, or at least, thought you knew. When it becomes people you've helped, supported, and encourage, it will be extremely painful. But again, stay focused on your assignment and do not let anything or anyone get in the way of it. Just smile and remember that you are destined for greatness...regardless of those who can't handle your success. Whatever situation you may find yourself in, do not allow people to hinder your progress. They won't be the first or the last to feel this way. Brush it off and keep moving forward...they aren't worth your energy!

Ask yourself:

- Are my haters masked or can I clearly see them?
- Can I handle the criticism that comes with success?
- Am I able to dismiss haters when I find out who they are?

My Commitment: _____

_____

_____

_____

_____

_____

_____

_____

_____

_____

_____

_____

_____

_____

_____

_____

_____

_____

_____

_____

_____

_____

_____

_____

_____

Instead of asking "<u>Y</u>" me, say "<u>Y</u>" not me?...

"If you never try, you'll never know what you are capable of." ~John Barrow

"Many are called, but few are chosen." During this lifetime, you will go through many trials and tribulations. We all do. Although it doesn't feel good, these tests truly come to make you stronger. They build you up each time so you are able to stand the tests as they continue to show up.

Robert Frost said, "Two roads diverged in the woods. I took the one less traveled...and that has made all the difference." Be that person! You can't be your absolute best when you're following a crowd. Set yourself apart from the rest and do your absolute best! Be bold and be fearless! You will not only be noticed, but you will be chosen. When you're chosen, don't ignore it. Step up and do your thing, do it right, and do it big!

Often times, people can see in you what you can't see in yourself. Pay attention to what they notice and study yourself. Your unique skill and ability is what will carry you high and set the standard for others. "WhY" you? YOU have what it takes, so make it happen!

Ask yourself:

+ Am I ready to be out front?
+ When called for a task. do I find an excuse to back out?
+ Do I really understand what it means to be bold and fearless?

My Commitment: _____

_____

_____

_____

_____

_____

_____

_____

_____

_____

_____

_____

_____

_____

_____

_____

_____

_____

Z

Zestfully walk into
your next phase of
life being proud of
who you are...

"In bad times and good, I have never lost my sense of
zest for life." ~Walt Disney

[77]

After all is said and done, when you accept the fact that you are <u>A</u>mazing, <u>B</u>eautiful, <u>C</u>harismatic, <u>D</u>aring, <u>E</u>nthusiastic, <u>F</u>earless, <u>G</u>racious, <u>H</u>umble, <u>I</u>nfinite, <u>J</u>oyous, <u>K</u>ind, <u>L</u>oving, <u>M</u>eaningful, <u>N</u>ecessary, <u>O</u>ptimistic, <u>P</u>ositive, ex<u>Q</u>uisite, <u>R</u>espectful, <u>S</u>harp, <u>T</u>eachable, <u>U</u>nwavering, <u>V</u>ibrant, <u>W</u>onderful, e<u>X</u>hilarating, and <u>Y</u>outhful, you can <u>Z</u>estfully walk into your next phase of life being the STAR that you are!

Keep your head up, your strut straight, and your confidence in full gear and you will be ready to CONQUER all that you desire!

Ask yourself:

- Does my walk and talk exude confidence?
- Do I know and am I ready for where I am headed?
- Is the world ready for me? If not, get ready. Here I come!

My Commitment: _____

_____

_____

_____

_____

_____

_____

_____

_____

_____

_____

_____

_____

_____

_____

_____

_____

_____

_____

_____

_____

_____

_____

_____

_____

_____

About the Author

 Ms. Deniece M. Fields is a 15-year, extremely dedicated and relentless educator who works in Urban Education and Leadership. She serves as a passionate Motivational Speaker and Professional Development Presenter for various groups and organizations throughout the United States. She has proudly served as a Lead Teacher, Curriculum Coordinator, Assistant Principal, Principal, District Support Coach, and Executive Director of educational institutions throughout the Midwest region, and has been recognized for her accomplishments in all of her roles. She is now taking her Leadership experiences and sharing them with other Leaders, both inside and outside of the Educational arena. Her professional development sessions, as well as her keynote speeches both motivate and inspire her audiences to do more to get the results they desire!

CPSIA information can be obtained at www.ICGtesting.com
Printed in the USA
BVOW11*0314170815

412952BV00008BB/25/P

9 780692 454107